Bread Cookbook

Delicious and Easy Bread Recipes

By
BookSumo Press

Published by
http://www.booksumo.com

ENJOY THE RECIPES?
KEEP ON COOKING
WITH 6 MORE FREE COOKBOOKS!

Visit our website and simply enter your email address to join the club and receive your 6 cookbooks.

http://booksumo.com/magnet

https://www.instagram.com/booksumopress/

https://www.facebook.com/booksumo/

LEGAL NOTES

Table of Contents

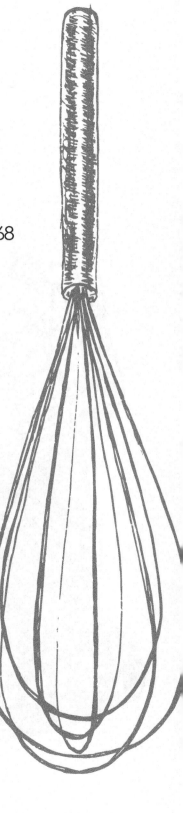

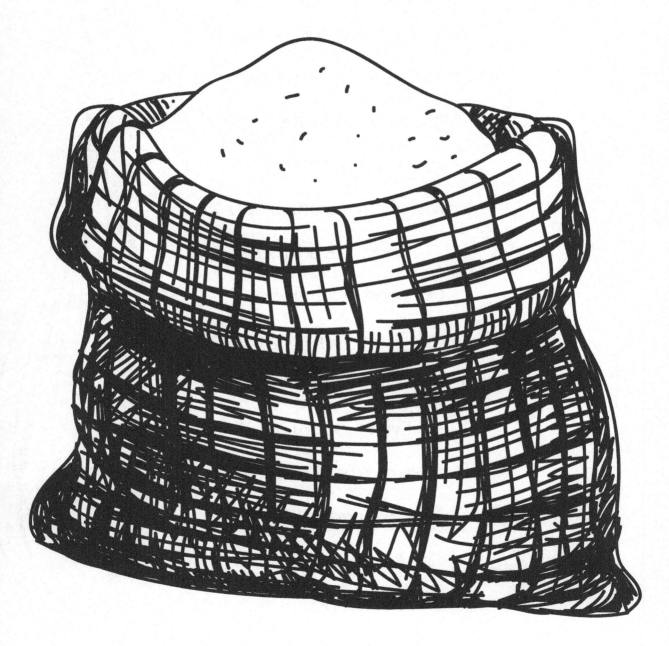

Banana Bread

🥣 Prep Time: 10 mins
🕐 Total Time: 1 hr 30 mins

Servings per Recipe: 12	
Calories	307 kcal
Fat	13.6 g
Carbohydrates	44.2g
Protein	3.8 g
Cholesterol	31 mg
Sodium	221 mg

Ingredients

2 eggs, beaten
1/3 C. buttermilk
1/2 C. vegetable oil
1 C. mashed bananas
1 1/2 C. white sugar
1 3/4 C. all-purpose flour

1 tsp baking soda
1/2 tsp salt
1/2 C. diced almonds
1/2 C. diced pistachios

Directions

1. Coat a bread pan with nonstick spray then set your oven to 325 degrees before doing anything else.
2. Get a bowl, combine: bananas, eggs, oil, and buttermilk.
3. Get a 2nd bowl, sift: salt, sugar, baking soda, and flour. Then combine in the nuts.
4. Now mix both bowls and enter the batter into your bread pan.
5. Cook everything in the oven for 80 mins.
6. Enjoy.

CINNAMON
Pumpkin Bread

Prep Time: 15 mins
Total Time: 1 hr 15 mins

Servings per Recipe: 36
Calories	247 kcal
Fat	10.3 g
Carbohydrates	36.8g
Protein	3 g
Cholesterol	31 mg
Sodium	231 mg

Ingredients

3 C. canned pumpkin puree
1 1/2 C. vegetable oil
4 C. white sugar
6 eggs
4 3/4 C. all-purpose flour
1 1/2 tsps baking powder
1 1/2 tsps baking soda

1 1/2 tsps salt
1 1/2 tsps ground cinnamon
1 1/2 tsps ground nutmeg
1 1/2 tsps ground cloves

Directions

1. Coat three bread pans with oil and flour then set your oven to 350 degrees before doing anything else.
2. Get a bowl, combine: eggs, pumpkin, sugar, and oil.
3. Stir the mix until it's smooth and even then add in: cloves, flour, nutmeg, baking powder, cinnamon, baking soda, and salt.
4. Form a smooth batter until by stirring the mix then enter everything into your bread pans.
5. Cook the contents in the oven for 55 mins.
6. Enjoy.

Vanilla
Date Walnut Bread

Prep Time: 40 mins
Total Time: 1 hr 40 mins

Servings per Recipe: 24

Calories	226 kcal
Fat	5.2 g
Carbohydrates	42.2g
Protein	3.9 g
Cholesterol	16 mg
Sodium	276 mg

Ingredients

1 1/2 C. dates, pitted and diced
2 1/4 C. boiling water
3 tsps baking soda
1 C. diced walnuts
2 C. white sugar
3 tbsps margarine

2 eggs, beaten
1 tsp salt
4 1/2 C. all-purpose flour
1 tsp vanilla extract

Directions

1. Coat two bread pans with oil then set your oven to 300 degrees before doing anything else.
2. Get a bowl, combine: boiling water and baking soda.
3. Stir the mix then add in your dates. Then let everything sit for 40 mins.
4. Now get a 2nd bowl, combine: butter and sugar. Mix these ingredients until they are creamy then add: salt, eggs, flour, vanilla, nuts, and dates.
5. Form the mix into a smooth batter then pour the batter into the pans.
6. Cook the bread for 60 mins.
7. Enjoy.

BANANA
Bread II

🥣 Prep Time: 15 mins
🕐 Total Time: 1 hr 45 mins

Servings per Recipe: 12
Calories   334 kcal
Fat   16.6 g
Carbohydrates   43.8g
Protein   5.3 g
Cholesterol   51 mg
Sodium   407 mg

Ingredients

cooking spray
2 C. all-purpose flour
1 tsp salt
1 tsp baking powder
1 tsp baking soda
1/2 C. butter, softened
3 ripe bananas, mashed

1 C. white sugar
2 large eggs
1/4 tsp vanilla extract
1 tbsp milk
1 C. diced walnuts
1/3 C. semisweet chocolate chips

Directions

1. Coat a bread pan with nonstick spray then set your oven to 325 degrees before doing anything else.
2. Get a bowl, combine: baking soda, flour, baking powder, and salt.
3. Get a 2nd bowl, mix, with an electric mixer: sugar and butter.
4. Combine in the bananas and continue mixing everything until it is all smooth.
5. Add the eggs into the mix one by one then add the milk and vanilla.
6. Continue mixing until you have a smooth batter then add the chocolate and walnuts.
7. Mix everything one last time.
8. Now combine both bowls, form a batter, and pour everything into your pan.
9. Cook the bread in the oven for 70 mins then let the bread lose its heat before removing it from the pan.
10. Enjoy.

Cinnamon
Pecan Pear Bread

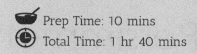 Prep Time: 10 mins

Total Time: 1 hr 40 mins

Servings per Recipe: 20	
Calories	279 kcal
Fat	13.1 g
Carbohydrates	38g
Protein	3.5 g
Cholesterol	28 mg
Sodium	196 mg

Ingredients

3 C. all-purpose flour
1/4 tsp baking powder
1 tsp baking soda
1 tsp salt
1 tbsp ground cinnamon
3/4 C. vegetable oil

3 eggs
2 C. white sugar
2 C. peeled shredded pears
1 C. diced pecans
2 tsps vanilla extract

Directions

1. Coat two loaf pans with oil and flour then set your oven to 325 degrees before doing anything else.
2. Get a bowl, combine: cinnamon, flour, salt, baking powder, and baking soda.
3. Get a 2nd bowl, combine: vanilla, oil, pecans, eggs, shredded pears, and sugar.
4. Now combine both bowls.
5. Pour this mix into your bread pans and cook the contents in the oven for 80 mins.
6. Let the bread lose its heat before removing it from the pan.
7. Enjoy.

MAGGIE'S
Persimmon Bread

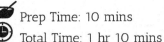 Prep Time: 10 mins

Total Time: 1 hr 10 mins

Servings per Recipe: 24	
Calories	292 kcal
Fat	13.4 g
Carbohydrates	41.1g
Protein	3.5 g
Cholesterol	31 mg
Sodium	262 mg

Ingredients

1 C. persimmon pulp
2 tsps baking soda
3 C. white sugar
1 C. vegetable oil
4 eggs
1 1/2 tsps ground cinnamon
1/2 tsp ground nutmeg

1 1/2 tsps salt
2/3 C. water
3 C. all-purpose flour
1 C. diced walnuts

Directions

1. Coat 3 bread pans with oil then set your oven to 350 degrees before doing anything else.
2. Get a bowl, combine: baking soda and persimmon pulp.
3. Leave the mix to sit for 10 mins.
4. Get a 2nd bowl, combine: salt, sugar, nutmeg, oil, cinnamon, and eggs.
5. Combine this mix until its smooth then combine both bowls.
6. Add in the water and flour then add the nuts.
7. Form a smooth batter and enter everything into your bread pans.
8. Cook the bread in the oven for 65 mins then let the leaves sit outside the oven for 15 mins before removing them from the pans.
9. Enjoy.

Caribbean Bread

Prep Time: 30 mins
Total Time: 3 hrs 20 mins

Servings per Recipe: 24
Calories	243 kcal
Fat	12.2 g
Carbohydrates	31.3g
Protein	3 g
Cholesterol	25 mg
Sodium	248 mg

Ingredients

3 C. all-purpose flour
2 tsps baking soda
1 1/2 tsps baking powder
1 tsp salt
1 tsp ground cinnamon
1 tsp pumpkin pie spice
3 eggs
1 C. vegetable oil
1 C. white sugar

1 C. light brown sugar
1/2 C. sour cream
2 tsps vanilla extract
3 C. grated unpeeled zucchini
1 (20 oz.) can crushed pineapple, well drained
1/2 C. shredded coconut

Directions

1. Coat two bread pans with oil then set your oven to 350 degrees before doing anything else.
2. Get a bowl, combine: pumpkin pie spice, flour, cinnamon, baking soda, salt, and baking powder.
3. Get a 2nd bowl, combine: brown sugar, eggs, white sugar, and oil.
4. Combine the mix until it is smooth then stir in: coconut, sour cream, pineapple, vanilla, and zucchini.
5. Now mix both bowls and enter the contents into your bread pan.
6. Cook the loaves in the oven for 55 mins then let the loaves sit for 15 mins before removing them from the pan.
7. Enjoy.

BANANA
Bread III

Prep Time: 10 mins
Total Time: 1 hr 10 mins

Servings per Recipe: 15
Calories	226 kcal
Fat	7.1 g
Carbohydrates	38.5g
Protein	3.1 g
Cholesterol	42 mg
Sodium	136 mg

Ingredients

1 1/2 C. white sugar
1/2 C. butter, softened
3 bananas, mashed
2 eggs
2 C. all-purpose flour
1/2 tsp baking soda
1/3 C. sour milk

1/4 tsp salt
1 tsp vanilla extract

Directions

1. Coat a bread pan with oil then set your oven to 350 degrees before doing anything else.
2. Get a bowl, combine: vanilla, sugar, salt, butter, milk, bananas, baking soda, flour, and eggs.
3. Stir this mix until it is smooth then enter everything into your pan.
4. Cook the bread for 1 hr in the oven.
5. Enjoy.

Buttermilk
Cornbread

Prep Time: 15 mins
Total Time: 55 mins

Servings per Recipe: 9

Calories	284 kcal
Fat	12.2 g
Carbohydrates	39.1g
Protein	4.8 g
Cholesterol	59 mg
Sodium	318 mg

Ingredients

1/2 C. butter
2/3 C. white sugar
2 eggs
1 C. buttermilk
1/2 tsp baking soda

1 C. cornmeal
1 C. all-purpose flour
1/2 tsp salt

Directions

1. Coat a bread pan with oil then set your oven to 375 degrees before doing anything else.
2. Begin to heat and stir your sugar in melted butter for 1 min then shut the heat and add in eggs, salt, flour, baking soda, cornmeal, and buttermilk.
3. Enter this mix into your bread pan and cook everything in the oven for 35 mins.
4. Let the bread cool before removing it from the pan.
5. Enjoy.

SOUR CREAM
Banana Bread

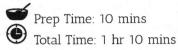 Prep Time: 10 mins
Total Time: 1 hr 10 mins

Servings per Recipe: 15
Calories	218 kcal
Fat	11.1 g
Carbohydrates	27.4g
Protein	3.2 g
Cholesterol	44 mg
Sodium	219 mg

Ingredients

1/2 C. butter, melted
1 C. white sugar
2 eggs
1 tsp vanilla extract
1 1/2 C. all-purpose flour
1 tsp baking soda
1/2 tsp salt

1/2 C. sour cream
1/2 C. diced walnuts
2 medium bananas, sliced

Directions

1. Coat a bread pan with oil then set your oven to 350 degrees before doing anything else.
2. Get a bowl, combine: sugar and melted butter.
3. Stir the mix then add in the vanilla and eggs.
4. Continue stirring everything until the mix is smooth then add in the salt, baking soda, and flour. Stir the mix again then add: the bananas, nuts, and sour cream.
5. Add the mix to the bread pan once it is smooth and even then cook everything in the oven for 1 hr.
6. Let the bread loose its heat before serving.
7. Enjoy.

Vanilla
Zucchini Bread

Prep Time: 15 mins
Total Time: 1 hr 45 mins

Servings per Recipe: 12	
Calories	461 kcal
Fat	19.9 g
Carbohydrates	66.8g
Protein	5.3 g
Cholesterol	46 mg
Sodium	281 mg

Ingredients

3 eggs, lightly beaten
1 C. vegetable oil
3 tsps vanilla extract
2 1/4 C. white sugar
2 C. shredded zucchini
3 C. all-purpose flour
1 tsp salt

1 tsp baking powder
1/4 tsp baking soda
1 tbsp ground cinnamon
1 pint fresh blueberries

Directions

1. Coat 4 mini loaf pans with oil and set your oven to 350 degrees before doing anything else.
2. Get a bowl, combine: sugar, eggs, vanilla, and oil.
3. Add in your zucchini and stir the mix before adding: cinnamon, flour, baking soda, salt, and baking powder.
4. Stir the mix then add the blueberries and place everything into the pans.
5. Cook the bread in the oven for 55 mins then let the bread cool before serving it.
6. Enjoy.

CLASSIC
Cornbread

Prep Time: 15 mins
Total Time: 50 mins

Servings per Recipe: 15
Calories	234 kcal
Fat	9.3 g
Carbohydrates	33.1g
Protein	4.9 g
Cholesterol	28 mg
Sodium	253 mg

Ingredients

1 1/2 C. cornmeal
2 1/2 C. milk
2 C. all-purpose flour
1 tbsp baking powder
1 tsp salt

2/3 C. white sugar
2 eggs
1/2 C. vegetable oil

Directions

1. Set your oven to 400 degrees before doing anything else.
2. Get a bowl, combine: milk, and cornmeal.
3. Let the contents sit for 12 mins then coat a baking pan with oil.
4. Get a 2nd bigger bowl, combine: sugar, flour, salt, and baking powder. Stir the mix then add in the oil, eggs, and cornmeal. Work this mix into a batter and continue stirring the batter for 2 mins.
5. Enter the batter into your baking pan and cook the bread in the oven for 32 mins.
6. Enjoy.

Rosemary
Bread

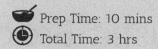
Prep Time: 10 mins
Total Time: 3 hrs

Servings per Recipe: 12
Calories	137 kcal
Fat	3.9 g
Carbohydrates	21.6g
Protein	3.6 g
Cholesterol	0 mg
Sodium	292 mg

Ingredients

1 C. water
3 tbsps olive oil
1 1/2 tsps white sugar
1 1/2 tsps salt
1/4 tsp Italian seasoning

1/4 tsp ground black pepper
1 tbsp dried rosemary
2 1/2 C. bread flour
1 1/2 tsps active dry yeast

Directions

1. Add the ingredients to your bread machine cook the bread on the white bread setting.
2. Let the machine finish, then serve the bread once it has cooled.
3. Enjoy.

EASY
Rustic Bread

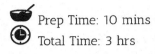 Prep Time: 10 mins
Total Time: 3 hrs

Servings per Recipe: 12
Calories	137 kcal
Fat	3.9 g
Carbohydrates	21.6g
Protein	3.6 g
Cholesterol	0 mg
Sodium	292 mg

Ingredients

1 C. water
3 tbsps olive oil
1 1/2 tsps white sugar
1 1/2 tsps salt
1/4 tsp Italian seasoning
1/4 tsp ground black pepper

1 tbsp dried rosemary
2 1/2 C. bread flour
2 tbsps tarragon
1 1/2 tsps active dry yeast

Directions

1. Add all the ingredients to your bread machine and set the machine to the white bread cycle.
2. Let the machine work and finis the cycle.
3. Once the bread is done let it cool before serving.
4. Enjoy.

Easy
Potato Flake Bread

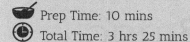 Prep Time: 10 mins
Total Time: 3 hrs 25 mins

Servings per Recipe: 15

Calories	162 kcal
Fat	1.8 g
Carbohydrates	31.6g
Protein	4.5 g
Cholesterol	< 1 mg
Sodium	< 339 mg

Ingredients

2 1/2 tsps active dry yeast
1/4 C. warm water (110 degrees F/45 degrees C)
1 tbsp white sugar
4 C. all-purpose flour
1/4 C. dry potato flakes
1/4 C. dry milk powder

2 tsps salt
3 tbsp diced chives
1/4 C. white sugar
2 tbsps margarine
1 C. warm water

Directions

1. Get a bowl, combine: sugar, 1/4 C. C. warm water, and yeast.
2. Let the mix stand for 20 mins.
3. Now add all the ingredients to your bread machine and set the machine to the basic / light crust setting.
4. Once the machine is done serve the bread.
5. Enjoy.

WHEAT
Bread

Prep Time: 20 mins
Total Time: 3 hrs

Servings per Recipe: 36
Calories   143 kcal
Fat   2.2 g
Carbohydrates   27.6g
Protein   4.1 g
Cholesterol   4 mg
Sodium   207 mg

Ingredients

3 C. warm water (110 degrees F/45 degrees C)
2 (.25 oz.) packages active dry yeast
1/3 C. honey
5 C. bread flour
3 tbsps butter, melted

1/3 C. honey
1 tbsp salt
3 1/2 C. whole wheat flour
2 tbsps butter, melted

Directions

1. Get a bowl, combine: 1/3 C. honey, warm water, and yeast. Stir the mix then add in your bread flour and stir the mix again.
2. Let the contents stand for 40 mins.
3. Now combine in salt, 1/3 C. of honey, and 3 tbsps melted butter. Stir the mix then add 2 more C. of wheat flour.
4. Knead your dough on a floured cutting board.
5. Work the dough until it's somewhat sticky.
6. You may need work in about 3 more C. of wheat flour to get the dough sticky.
7. Add your dough to an oiled bowl and coat the dough with oil by turning it in the bowl.
8. Cover the bowl with a damp kitchen towel and let the dough sit until it has doubled in size.
9. Now set your oven to 350 degrees before doing anything else.
10. Work down the dough and divide it into 3 pieces.
11. Place your pieces of dough into loaf pans that have been coated with oil then let the dough sit for 30 mins.
12. Cook your bread, in the oven for 27 mins. Then coat each piece of bread with 2 tbsp of melted butter.
13. Enjoy.

Italian Bread

🥄 Prep Time: 20 mins
🕐 Total Time: 3 hrs

Servings per Recipe: 15
Calories	93 kcal
Fat	1.6 g
Carbohydrates	16.3g
Protein	3 g
Cholesterol	9 mg
Sodium	179 mg

Ingredients

3 C. unbleached flour
1 tbsp light brown sugar
1 1/3 C. warm water (110 degrees F/45 degrees C)
1 1/2 tsps salt
1 1/2 tbsps olive oil
1 (.25 oz.) package active dry yeast

1 egg
1 tbsp water
2 tbsps cornmeal

Directions

1. Add the following to your bread machine: yeast, flour, olive oil, brown sugar, salt, and warm water.
2. Set the machine to the dough cycle and let the machine work.
3. Now set your oven to 375 degrees before doing anything else.
4. Get a pizza stone and put it in the oven as it gets hot. Let the oven preheat for 40 mins.
5. Now knead your dough on a floured cutting board then divide the dough into 2 pieces and form each piece into a loaf. Place a moist kitchen towel over the dough and let them sit for 40 mins.
6. Get a bowl, combine: 1 tbsp water and egg.
7. After the dough has sat coat each piece with the egg mix.
8. With a sharp knife cut each piece of dough in half lengthwise. Then place the dough on the pizza stone.
9. Cook your bread in the oven for 35 to 40 mins.
10. Enjoy.

MOZZARELLA
and Parmesan Bread

 Prep Time: 15 mins

Total Time: 2 hrs 55 mins

Servings per Recipe: 10

Calories	233 kcal
Fat	10.1 g
Carbohydrates	22.5g
Protein	11.4 g
Cholesterol	38 mg
Sodium	540 mg

Ingredients

1 (1 lb) loaf frozen bread dough, thawed
1 egg, whisked
4 oz. sliced pepperoni sausage
1 C. shredded mozzarella cheese

1/4 C. grated Parmesan cheese
1 1/2 tsps Italian seasoning

Directions

1. Get a cookie sheet and coat it with oil then set your oven to 375 degrees before doing anything else.
2. Shape your dough into a rectangle then top it with the whisked eggs. Place the mozzarella and pepperoni on top of the dough and add the parmesan over everything.
3. Finally add your Italian seasoning and roll the dough. Crimp the seam to create a seal and place the rolled dough on the cookie sheet.
4. Cook everything in the oven for 45 mins.
5. Enjoy.

Russian
Bread

Prep Time: 15 mins
Total Time: 3 hrs 15 mins

Servings per Recipe: 15
Calories	172 kcal
Fat	2.7 g
Carbohydrates	32.6g
Protein	4.8 g
Cholesterol	0 mg
Sodium	222 mg

Ingredients

1 1/2 C. water
2 tbsps cider vinegar
2 1/2 C. bread flour
1 C. rye flour
1 tsp salt
2 tbsps margarine
2 tbsps dark corn syrup

1 tbsp brown sugar
3 tbsps unsweetened cocoa powder
1 tsp instant coffee granules
1 tbsp caraway seed
1/4 tsp fennel seed (optional)
2 tsps active dry yeast

Directions

1. Add all the ingredients to your bread machine and set the machine to the regular crust setting.
2. Let the bread cool before cutting it into 12 pieces.
3. Enjoy.

CINNAMON
Raisin Bread

Prep Time: 15 mins
Total Time: 1 hr

Servings per Recipe: 15
Calories	418 kcal
Fat	17.7 g
Carbohydrates	61.5g
Protein	5.3 g
Cholesterol	< 1 mg
Sodium	< 746 mg

Ingredients

3 (12 oz.) packages refrigerated biscuit
dough
1 C. white sugar
2 tsps ground cinnamon
1/2 C. margarine

1 C. packed brown sugar
1/2 C. diced walnuts (optional)
1/2 C. raisins

Directions

1. Coat a Bundt pan with oil then set your oven to 350 degrees before doing anything else.
2. Get a big bowl, combine: cinnamon and sugar.
3. Slice your biscuits into 4 pieces each then add 7 pieces to your sugar mix and toss the biscuits.
4. Layer your coated biscuits in the Bundt pan then keep coating and tossing more biscuits.
5. As you are adding more biscuits add in your nuts and raisins in between.
6. Set your oven to 350 degrees before doing anything else.
7. Now begin to heat your brown sugar and margarine in a saucepan let this mix boil for 60 secs then coat your biscuits with it.
8. Cook everything in the oven for 40 mins. Let the bread loose its heat then break it into pieces for serving.
9. Enjoy.

Easy Focaccia

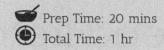

Prep Time: 20 mins
Total Time: 1 hr

Servings per Recipe: 12

Calories	171 kcal
Fat	5.8 g
Carbohydrates	23.4g
Protein	6 g
Cholesterol	5 mg
Sodium	252 mg

Ingredients

2 3/4 C. all-purpose flour
1 tsp salt
1 tsp white sugar
1 tbsp active dry yeast
1 tsp garlic powder
1 tsp dried oregano
1 tsp dried thyme
1/2 tsp dried basil
1 pinch ground black pepper

1 tbsp vegetable oil
1 C. water
2 tbsps olive oil
1 tbsp grated Parmesan cheese
1 C. mozzarella

Directions

1. Get a bowl, combine: black pepper, flour, basil, salt, thyme, sugar, oregano, yeast, and garlic powder. Combine the mix until it is smooth then add in the water and the veggie oil.
2. Work your dough on a floured cutting board and knead it until it's smooth.
3. Place the dough in a greased bowl and turn the dough to coat it with oil.
4. Place a damp kitchen towel around the bowl and let the dough sit for 25 mins.
5. Now set your oven to 450 degrees before doing anything else.
6. Punch down the dough and layer it on a cookie sheet that has been coated with oil.
7. Flatten the dough in a rectangle and top it with olive oil then with mozzarella and parmesan.
8. Cook everything in the oven for 20 mins.
9. Enjoy.

CLASSICAL
Bread from France

 Prep Time: 25 mins
Total Time: 2 hrs 40 mins

Servings per Recipe: 30
Calories	94 kcal
Fat	0.3 g
Carbohydrates	< 19.5g
Protein	2.9 g
Cholesterol	0 mg
Sodium	119 mg

Ingredients

6 C. all-purpose flour
2 1/2 (.25 oz.) packages active dry
yeast
2 C. warm water (110 degrees F/45
degrees C)

1 1/2 tsps salt
1 tbsp cornmeal
1 egg white
1 tbsp water

Directions

1. Get a bowl, combine: salt, yeast, and 2 C. of flour. Add in 2 C. of water and mix everything. Then combine in the flour and form a dough.
2. Once you have formed a dough knead it on a floured cutting board until it becomes somewhat stiff. Continue working the dough for 10 more mins.
3. Form the dough into a large ball and place it in an oiled bowl. Place a covering on the bowl (damp kitchen towel) and let the dough sit for an hour or until it has doubled in size.
4. Work your dough down in size and break it into two pieces.
5. Knead the pieces on a floured cutting board then place a covering on the dough again and let it sit for 15 mins.
6. Shape each piece of dough into a rectangle and roll it. Apply some water to the edge of your bread and seal it.
7. Now combine 1 tbsp of water with your egg whites.
8. Coat a cookie sheet with oil and cornmeal then place your pieces of dough on the sheet.
9. Coat the bread with the egg white mix and place a damp kitchen towel over the bread.
10. Now set your oven to 375 degrees before doing anything else.
11. Let the bread sit for 37 mins. Then make 4 diagonal incisions in your dough and cook everything in the oven for 22 mins.
12. Top the bread again with more egg whites and continue cooking everything for 17 more mins. Enjoy.

Naan
(Indian Style Bread)

Prep Time: 30 mins
Total Time: 3 hrs

Servings per Recipe: 14
Calories	211 kcal
Fat	4.5 g
Carbohydrates	36g
Protein	6.1 g
Cholesterol	22 mg
Sodium	364 mg

Ingredients

1 (.25 oz.) package active dry yeast
1 C. warm water
1/4 C. white sugar
3 tbsps milk
1 egg, beaten

2 tsps salt
4 1/2 C. bread flour
2 tsps minced garlic (optional)
1/4 C. butter, melted

Directions

1. Get a bowl, combine: warm water and yeast. Let the mix sit for 15 mins.
2. Now add in flour, sugar, salt, egg, and milk.
3. Shape the mix into a dough and knead it for 10 mins on a floured cutting board. Layer the dough in an oiled bowl and place a damp kitchen towel over the bowl.
4. Let the dough sit for 60 mins.
5. Knead the dough again and work in your garlic.
6. Then form small golf ball size pieces from the dough.
7. Place the balls on a cookie sheet, place a towel on top of the dough, and let everything sit for 40 mins.
8. Now get a grill hot.
9. Take each ball and roll it out into a think circle.
10. Coat your grill with oil and cook the dough for 3 mins then coat the bread with butter and flip it.
11. Coat the opposite side with butter and cook the naan for 2 more mins.
12. Enjoy.

EASY
Cinnamon Rolls

Prep Time: 20 mins
Total Time: 3 hrs

Servings per Recipe: 12	
Calories	525 kcal
Fat	18.6 g
Carbohydrates	82g
Protein	9 g
Cholesterol	64 mg
Sodium	388 mg

Ingredients

1 C. warm milk (110 degrees F/45 degrees C)
2 eggs, room temperature
1/3 C. margarine, melted
4 1/2 C. bread flour
1 tsp salt
1/2 C. white sugar
2 1/2 tsps bread machine yeast
1 C. brown sugar, packed

2 1/2 tbsps ground cinnamon
1/3 C. butter, softened
1 (3 oz.) package cream cheese, softened
1/4 C. butter, softened
1 1/2 C. confectioners' sugar
1/2 tsp vanilla extract
1/8 tsp salt

Directions

1. Add all the ingredients to your bread machine except the cinnamon and sugar.
2. Set the bread machine to the dough cycle and let it work.
3. Once the dough has been formed knead it on a floured surface and let it sit in a bowl until it doubles in size.
4. Get a bowl, combine: cinnamon and brown sugar.
5. Now form a 16x21 inch rectangle.
6. Coat the dough with 1/3 C. of butter and then top it with the cinnamon mix.
7. Divide the dough into 12 pieces and shape each piece into a roll.
8. Layer the rolls on an oiled baking pan and place a covering on the pan.
9. Let the dough sit for 40 mins.
10. Now set your oven to 400 degrees and cook the rolls in oven for 20 mins in the oven once it is hot.
11. As the rolls cook get a bowl, combine: salt, cream cheese, vanilla, 1/4 C. butter, and confectioners. Coat your rolls with the cream cheese mix.
12. Enjoy.

Rolls
for Dinner-Time

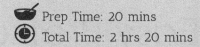 Prep Time: 20 mins

Total Time: 2 hrs 20 mins

Servings per Recipe: 16
Calories	192 kcal
Fat	7.5 g
Carbohydrates	27.1g
Protein	3.9 g
Cholesterol	30 mg
Sodium	202 mg

Ingredients

1/2 C. warm water (110 degrees F/45 degrees C)
1/2 C. warm milk
1 egg
1/3 C. butter, softened
1/3 C. white sugar

1 tsp salt
3 3/4 C. all-purpose flour
1 (.25 oz.) package active dry yeast
1/4 C. butter, softened

Directions

1. Add the following to your bread machine: yeast, water, flour, milk, salt, egg, sugar, and 1/3 C. butter.
2. Set the machine to the dough / knead cycle to form a dough.
3. Once the dough is finished break it into two pieces and roll each piece into a 12 inch circle.
4. Coach each piece with 1/4 C. butter. Then slice each of the halves into 8 pieces.
5. Roll each of the 8 pieces tightly then layer everything on a baking sheet.
6. Place a kitchen towel covering over everything and let the dough sit for 60 mins.
7. Now set your oven to 400 degrees before doing anything else.
8. Once the oven is hot cook the bread in the oven for 12 mins.
9. Enjoy.

MAGGIE'S
Easy Pretzels

Prep Time: 2 hrs
Total Time: 2 hrs 20 mins

Servings per Recipe: 12
Calories	237 kcal
Fat	1.7 g
Carbohydrates	48.9g
Protein	5.9 g
Cholesterol	0 mg
Sodium	4681 mg

Ingredients

4 tsps active dry yeast
1 tsp white sugar
1 1/4 C. warm water (110 degrees F/45 degrees C)
5 C. all-purpose flour
1/2 C. white sugar

1 1/2 tsps salt
1 tbsp vegetable oil
1/2 C. baking soda
4 C. hot water
1/4 C. kosher salt, for topping

Directions

1. Get a bowl, combine: 1 1/4 C. warm water, yeast, 1 tsp sugar. Leave the mix for 12 mins.
2. Get a 2nd bigger bowl, combine: salt, flour, and half C. sugar. Combine in the oil and stir the mix until its smooth.
3. Now combine both bowls and make a dough.
4. Knead the mix for 10 mins and if the dough is too dry add a tbsp of water.
5. Get a 3rd bowl and coat it with oil then place the dough in the bowl and turn the dough to get it oily.
6. Place a covering of plastic around the bowl and let the dough sit for 60 mins.
7. Now set your oven to 450 degrees before doing anything else.
8. Coat two cookie sheets with oil.
9. Get a 4th big bowl and combine 4 C. of hot water and baking soda.
10. Now grab your dough and divide it into 12 pieces.
11. Roll each piece into a long rope then form it into a pretzel shape.
12. Now coat each pretzel with the baking soda mix then layer everything on your cookie sheets.
13. Top the dough with your kosher salt and cook everything in the oven for 10 mins.
14. Enjoy.

Parmesan Poppers

Prep Time: 10 mins
Total Time: 25 mins

Servings per Recipe: 8
Calories	157 kcal
Fat	9.5 g
Carbohydrates	15.3g
Protein	2.9 g
Cholesterol	13 mg
Sodium	400 mg

Ingredients

3 tbsps melted butter
1/4 tsp dill weed
1/4 tsp celery seed
1/4 tsp minced onion
1 tbsp grated Parmesan cheese

1 (10 oz.) can refrigerated biscuit dough, separated and cut into half circles
1 tbsp grated Parmesan cheese

Directions

1. Set your oven to 425 degrees before doing anything else.
2. Get a pie dish and add your melted butter to it.
3. Get a bowl, combine: 1 tbsp parmesan, dill, onion, and celery seed. Add this to the melted butter.
4. In the middle of your pie dish add one biscuit then layer your other biscuits around the first one.
5. Now add a topping of parmesan (1 tbsp) over everything.
6. Cook the mix in the oven for 17 mins.
7. Enjoy.

CRANBERRY
Bread

Prep Time: 15 mins
Total Time: 1 hr 5 mins

Servings per Recipe: 12
Calories	194
Fat	6.1g
Cholesterol	16mg
Sodium	265mg
Carbohydrates	32.1g
Protein	3.6g

Ingredients

2 C. all-purpose flour
½ tsp baking soda
1½ tsp baking powder
¾ tsp salt
1 egg
¾ C. white sugar

2 tbsp vegetable oil
¾ C. fresh orange juice
1 C. cranberries, chopped
½ C. walnuts, chopped
1 tbsp fresh orange zest, grated finely

Directions

1. Set your oven to 350 degrees F. Oil a bread pan.
2. In a large bowl, mix together flour, baking soda, baking powder and salt.
3. In another bowl, add egg, sugar, oil and orange juice and beat till well combined.
4. Add egg mixture into flour mixture and mix till well combined.
5. Fold in cranberries, walnuts and orange zest.
6. Transfer the mixture into prepared bread pan.
7. Bake for about 50 minutes or till a toothpick inserted in the center comes out clean.
8. Let the bread cool for 10 minutes before removing from pan.
9. Enjoy.

Easy
Portuguese Bread

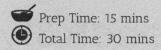
Prep Time: 15 mins
Total Time: 30 mins

Servings per Recipe: 16
Calories	118 kcal
Fat	5.9 g
Carbohydrates	14.3g
Protein	2 g
Cholesterol	< 1 mg
Sodium	< 169 mg

Ingredients

2 C. all-purpose flour
3 tsps baking powder
1/2 tsp salt
2 tbsps white sugar

3/4 C. milk
1 quart vegetable oil for frying

Directions

1. Get a bowl, combine: sugar, flour, salt, and baking powder.
2. Combine in the milk and stir the contents into a dough.
3. Shape the mix into small balls. Then flatten them on a working surface.
4. Each piece should have half an inch of thickness.
5. Now fry everything in hot oil until brown, then flip, and fry again.
6. Enjoy.

CLASSICAL
French Style Bread

 Prep Time: 25 mins
Total Time: 2 hrs 40 mins

Servings per Recipe: 30
Calories	94 kcal
Fat	0.3 g
Carbohydrates	19.5g
Protein	2.9 g
Cholesterol	0 mg
Sodium	119 mg

Ingredients

6 C. all-purpose flour
2 1/2 (.25 oz.) packages active dry
yeast
1 1/2 tsps salt
2 C. warm water (110 degrees F/45
degrees C)

1 tbsp cornmeal
1 egg white
1 tbsp water

Directions

1. Get bowl, mix: salt, flour (2 C.), warm water (2 C.), and yeast.
2. Use a mixer to combine the contents and then add in the rest of the flour, while continuing to stir.
3. For 12 mins knead this dough then add it to a bowl that has been coated with oil.
4. Place a covering over the bowl and let the dough rise until it has become twice its original size.
5. Now break the dough into 2 pieces and let it sit for another 12 mins.
6. Make sure you cover the dough again.
7. Shape the dough pieces into two large rectangles.
8. Place the doughs onto a baking sheet and top them with cornmeal and then brush them with 1 tbsp of water and some whisked egg whites.
9. Set your oven to 375 degrees before doing anything else.
10. Place of covering, again on the dough and let it sit for 37 mins.
11. Divide the dough in 4 pieces and cook the pieces for 22 mins in the oven.
12. Top the bread with more egg white and water.
13. Continue cooking for 17 more mins.
14. Let the bread cool before serving. Enjoy.

Portuguese Bread

🥣 Prep Time: 5 mins
🕐 Total Time: 3 hrs 5 mins

Servings per Recipe: 16
Calories   179 kcal
Fat   3.2 g
Carbohydrates   31.7g
Protein   5.6 g
Cholesterol   17 mg
Sodium   181 mg

Ingredients

1 C. milk
1 egg
2 tbsps margarine
1/3 C. white sugar

3/4 tsp salt
3 C. bread flour
2 1/2 tsps active dry yeast

Directions

1. To make this bread grab your bread maker. Enter the following into it: yeast, milk, flour, beaten eggs, salt, and margarine.
2. Set the bread machine to its basic cycle and let the machine go.
3. Let the bread sit for 10 mins before serving.
4. Enjoy.

SPICY
Jalapeno
Cornbread

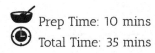 Prep Time: 10 mins
Total Time: 35 mins

Servings per Recipe: 12
Calories	189 kcal
Fat	7.4 g
Carbohydrates	28.2g
Protein	3.1 g
Cholesterol	17 mg
Sodium	354 mg

Ingredients

1 C. all-purpose flour
1 C. yellow cornmeal
2/3 C. white sugar
1 tsp salt
1/2 tsp cayenne
1 tbsp diced jalapeno, seeds removed

3 1/2 tsps baking powder
1 egg
1 C. milk
1/3 C. vegetable oil

Directions

1. Coat a loaf pan with nonstick spray then set your oven to 400 degrees before doing anything else.
2. Get a bowl, combine: baking powder, flour, salt, cayenne, sugar, and cornmeal. Stir the mix then add in: veggie oil, eggs, milk, and jalapenos.
3. Form the mix into a smooth batter then enter everything into your pan.
4. Cook the bread in the oven 30 mins.
5. Enjoy.

Peanut Butter Banana Almond Bread

🥣 Prep Time: 20 mins
🕐 Total Time: 1 hr 30 mins

Servings per Recipe: 24
Calories   232 kcal
Fat   11.9 g
Carbohydrates   29.7g
Protein   3.2 g
Cholesterol   51 mg
Sodium   268 mg

Ingredients

2 C. all-purpose flour
1 tsp salt
2 tsps baking soda
1 C. butter or margarine
1/2 C. peanut butter
2 C. white sugar

2 C. mashed overripe bananas
4 eggs, beaten
1 C. diced peanuts
1/2 C. diced roasted almonds

Directions

1. Coat two loaf pans with oil then set your oven to 350 degrees before doing anything else.
2. Get a bowl, sift: salt and flour.
3. Get a 2nd bowl, combine: sugar and butter. Stir this mix until it is creamy then add in: nuts, bananas, eggs, and peanut butter.
4. Now combine both bowls then form the mix into a smooth batter. Add the batter to your loaf pans then cook the bread in the oven for 65 mins. Allow the bread to lose its heat before removing it from the pan, then place the loaves in the fridge for 1 hr.
5. Enjoy.

RUSTIC
Cornbread

Prep Time: 15 mins
Total Time: 50 mins

Servings per Recipe: 15
Calories	234 kcal
Fat	9.3 g
Carbohydrates	33.1g
Protein	4.9 g
Cholesterol	28 mg
Sodium	253 mg

Ingredients

1 1/2 C. cornmeal
2 1/2 C. milk
2 C. all-purpose flour
1 tbsp baking powder
1 tsp cinnamon
1 tsp salt

2/3 C. white sugar
2 eggs
1/2 C. vegetable oil

Directions

1. Set your oven to 400 degrees before doing anything else.
2. Get a bowl, combine: milk, and cornmeal. Leave the mix for 10 mins.
3. Get a 2nd bowl, combine: sugar, flour, salt, baking powder, and cinnamon. Stir the mix then add in the oil and eggs.
4. Combine both bowls and form a smooth batter.
5. Enter the batter into your pan and cook the bread in the oven for 40 mins.
6. Enjoy.

Classical
Bread

Prep Time: 10 mins
Total Time: 3 hrs

Servings per Recipe: 12
Calories	174 kcal
Fat	5.2 g
Carbohydrates	27.1g
Protein	4.3 g
Cholesterol	0 mg
Sodium	195 mg

Ingredients

1 C. warm water (110 degrees F/45 degrees C)
2 tbsp white sugar
1 (.25 oz.) package bread machine yeast

1/4 C. vegetable oil
3 C. bread flour
1 tsp salt

Directions

1. In the pan of the bread machine, place water, sugar and yeast.
2. Let the yeast dissolve and foam for about 10 minutes.
3. Add the oil, flour and salt to the yeast.
4. Select the Basic or White Bread setting and press Start.

POPPY SEED
Bagels

Prep Time: 30 mins
Total Time: 3 hrs 55 mins

Servings per Recipe: 9

Calories	215 kcal
Fat	2.1 g
Carbohydrates	41.9g
Protein	6.8 g
Cholesterol	0 mg
Sodium	405 mg

Ingredients

1 C. warm water (110 degrees F/45 degrees C)
1 1/2 tsp salt
2 tbsp white sugar
3 C. bread flour
2 1/4 tsp active dry yeast

3 quarts boiling water
3 tbsp white sugar
1 tbsp cornmeal
1 egg white
3 tbsp poppy seeds

Directions

1. In the bread machine pan, place the water, salt, sugar, flour and yeast in the order recommended by the manufacturer.
2. Select the Dough setting.
3. When cycle is complete, place the dough rest on a lightly floured surface.
4. Meanwhile, in a large pan, add 3 quarts of the water and bring to a boil.
5. Stir in 3 tbsp of the sugar.
6. Cut dough into 9 equal portions and roll each portion into a small ball.
7. Flatten the balls and with your thumb, poke a hole in the center of each ball.
8. Spin the dough on your thumb to enlarge the hole and to even out the dough around the hole.
9. With a clean cloth, cover the bagels and keep aside for about 10 minutes.
10. Set your oven to 375 degrees F and sprinkle the cornmeal in an ungreased baking sheet.
11. Carefully transfer bagels into the boiling water and cook for about 1 minute, turning once in the middle way. Drain briefly on clean towel.
12. Arrange boiled bagels on baking sheet.
13. Glaze the tops with the egg white and sprinkle with your favorite toppings.
14. Cook in the oven for about 20-25 minutes.

Easy Homemade Challah

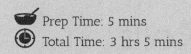

Prep Time: 5 mins
Total Time: 3 hrs 5 mins

Servings per Recipe: 12

Calories	184 kcal
Fat	4.4 g
Carbohydrates	30g
Protein	5.9 g
Cholesterol	32 mg
Sodium	341 mg

Ingredients

3/4 C. milk
2 eggs
3 tbsp margarine
3 C. bread flour

1/4 C. white sugar
1 1/2 tsp salt
1 1/2 tsp active dry yeast

Directions

1. In the bread machine pan, place all the ingredients in the order recommended by the manufacturer.
2. Select the Basic Bread and Light Crust settings.
3. Press the Start.

DINNER
Rolls

Prep Time: 1 hr 20 mins
Total Time: 1 hr 35 mins

Servings per Recipe: 12
Calories	165 kcal
Fat	2.5 g
Carbohydrates	29.5g
Protein	5.6 g
Cholesterol	6 mg
Sodium	227 mg

Ingredients

3 C. bread flour
3 tbsp white sugar
1 tsp salt
1/4 C. dry milk powder
1 C. warm water (110 degrees F/45 degrees C)

2 tbsp butter, softened
1 (.25 oz.) package active dry yeast
1 egg white
2 tbsp water

Directions

1. In the bread machine pan, place the bread flour, sugar, salt, milk powder, water, butter, and yeast in the order recommended by the manufacturer.
2. Select the Dough setting and press Start.
3. Remove the risen dough from the machine and place onto a lightly floured surface.
4. Divide the dough into twelve equal portions and form into rounds.
5. Place the rounds onto the lightly greased baking sheets.
6. With damp cloth, cover the rolls and keep aside for about 40 minutes.
7. Meanwhile, set your oven to 350 degrees F.
8. In a small bowl, mix together the egg white and 2 tbsp of the water.
9. Coat the rolls with egg mixture lightly.
10. Cook in the oven for about 15 minutes.

Pizza Dough

Prep Time: 10 mins
Total Time: 2 hrs 34 mins

Servings per Recipe: 6
Calories	262 kcal
Fat	4.4 g
Carbohydrates	46 g
Protein	6.2 g
Cholesterol	10 mg
Sodium	418 mg

Ingredients

1 C. flat beer
2 tbsp butter
2 tbsp sugar
1 tsp salt

2 1/2 C. all-purpose flour
2 1/4 tsp yeast

Directions

1. In the bread machine pan, place the beer, butter, sugar, salt, flour, and yeast in the order recommended by the manufacturer.
2. Select the Dough setting and press Start.
3. Remove the dough from bread machine after the cycle is completed.
4. Set your oven to 400 degrees F.
5. Roll the dough to cover a prepared pizza pan.
6. Lightly, brush the pizza dough with the olive oil.
7. Cover and keep aside for about 15 minutes.
8. Spread the sauce and toppings on the top of the dough.
9. Cook in the oven for about 24 minutes.

EASY
Homemade Calzones

 Prep Time: 30 mins

Total Time: 1 hr 20 mins

Servings per Recipe: 4
Calories	659 kcal
Fat	21 g
Carbohydrates	86.9g
Protein	28.2 g
Cholesterol	54 mg
Sodium	1442 mg

Ingredients

1 1/4 C. water
2 tsp active dry yeast
1 1/2 tbsp white sugar
3 C. bread flour
1 tsp salt
1 tsp powdered milk

3/4 C. sliced Italian sausage
3/4 C. pizza sauce
1 1/4 C. shredded mozzarella cheese
2 tbsp butter, melted

Directions

1. In the bread machine pan, place the water, yeast, sugar, flour, salt and powdered milk in the order recommended by the manufacturer.
2. Select the Dough cycle.
3. After cycle is completed, roll the dough on a lightly floured surface.
4. Meanwhile, heat a large skillet on medium heat and cook the sausage for about 8-10 minutes.
5. Drain the excess fat and reserve.
6. Set your oven to 350 degrees F.
7. Shape the dough into a 16x10-inch rectangle.
8. Arrange the dough onto a lightly greased cookie sheet and place the pizza sauce lengthwise down the center of the dough, followed by the sausage and cheese.
9. Make diagonal cuts 1 1/2-inches apart down each long side of the dough rectangle, cutting to within 1/2 inch of the filling.
10. Criss-cross cut strips of dough over the filling and seal the edges with the wet fingers.
11. Coat the top of calzone with the melted butter.
12. Cook in the oven for about 35-45 minutes.
13. Remove from the oven and cool for about 5 minutes before slicing.

White Bread
101

Prep Time: 5 mins
Total Time: 3 hrs 5 mins

Servings per Recipe: 6

Calories	124 kcal
Fat	2.6 g
Carbohydrates	20.9g
Protein	3.8 g
Cholesterol	17 mg
Sodium	243 mg

Ingredients

1 C. water
1 extra large egg, beaten
2 tbsp dry milk powder
1 tbsp white sugar
2 tbsp vegetable oil
1 1/2 tsp salt

1 C. bread flour
2 C. all-purpose flour
1 1/4 tsp active dry yeast

Directions

1. In the bread machine pan, place all the ingredients in the order recommended by the manufacturer.
2. Select the Basic bread setting and Normal Crust.

NEW YORK STYLE
Pizza Crust

Prep Time: 10 mins
Total Time: 1 hr 30 mins

Servings per Recipe: 12
Calories	136 kcal
Fat	1.2 g
Carbohydrates	26.5g
Protein	4.2 g
Cholesterol	0 mg
Sodium	195 mg

Ingredients

1 1/4 C. warm water (110 degrees F / 45 degrees C)
2 C. all-purpose flour
1 C. semolina flour
1/2 tsp white sugar
1 tsp salt

2 tsp olive oil
2 tsp active dry yeast

Directions

1. In the bread machine pan, place all the ingredients in the order recommended by the manufacturer.
2. Select the Dough cycle.
3. Remove after Rise cycle and use with your favorite pizza recipe.

Sourdough
101

Prep Time: 10 mins
Total Time: 1 hr 30 mins

Servings per Recipe: 12
Calories	177 kcal
Fat	4.8 g
Carbohydrates	28.6g
Protein	4.8 g
Cholesterol	6 mg
Sodium	228 mg

Ingredients

3/4 C. water
3/4 C. sour cream, room temperature
1 tbsp vegetable oil
1 1/8 tsp salt
2 1/2 C. bread flour
1/2 C. barley flour

2 tbsp dry potato flakes
2 tbsp white sugar
1 1/2 tsp active dry yeast

Directions

1. In the bread machine pan, place all the ingredients in the order recommended by the manufacturer.
2. Select the White Bread setting and press Start.

ALMOND
Flour Almond Oil Bread

 Prep Time: 10 mins
Total Time: 3 hrs 10 mins

Servings per Recipe: 12
Calories	117 kcal
Fat	1.9 g
Carbohydrates	22g
Protein	4.6 g
Cholesterol	0 mg
Sodium	206 mg

Ingredients

1 1/4 C. water
4 tsp almond oil
1 tsp salt
1/4 C. honey
1 C. almond flour
2 C. whole wheat flour

1/4 C. vital wheat gluten
1 tsp xanthan gum
1 (.25 oz.) package dry yeast

Directions

1. In the bread machine pan, place the water, almond oil, salt, honey, almond flour, whole wheat flour, vital wheat gluten, xanthan gum, and yeast in the order recommended by the manufacturer.

2. Follow the manufacturers' directions for a 2 lb. loaf.

December's
Applesauce and Cardamom Bread

Prep Time: 10 mins
Total Time: 2 hrs 45 mins

Servings per Recipe: 12	
Calories	161 kcal
Fat	1.2 g
Carbohydrates	32.1g
Protein	5.3 g
Cholesterol	16 mg
Sodium	60 mg

Ingredients

1/2 C. milk
1 egg
1/4 C. honey
1/4 C. unsweetened applesauce
1/4 tsp salt
3 C. bread flour

1/2 tsp ground cardamom
2 tsp active dry yeast

Directions

1. In the bread machine pan, place all the ingredients in the order recommended by the manufacturer.
2. Select the Dough cycle and press Start.
3. After the cycle is completed, remove the dough and knead slightly.
4. Form into a loaf shape and place into a greased 9x5-inch bread loaf pan.
5. Cover and keep in a warm place for about 45 minutes.
6. Set your oven to 350 degrees F.
7. Uncover the loaf, and coat the top with the water.
8. Cook in the oven for about 40-45 minutes.
9. Allow to cool for 10 minutes before removing from the pan.
10. Cool for about 1 hour before slicing.

GARLIC
and Rosemary
Bread

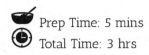 Prep Time: 5 mins
Total Time: 3 hrs

Servings per Recipe: 12
Calories	166 kcal
Fat	5.1 g
Carbohydrates	25.2g
Protein	4.3 g
Cholesterol	0 mg
Sodium	99 mg

Ingredients

1 C. lukewarm water
2 tbsp olive oil
1/2 tsp salt
2 tsp chopped garlic
1 tbsp chopped fresh rosemary
3 C. bread flour

1 1/2 tsp active dry yeast
2 tbsp olive oil
1 1/2 tsp chopped fresh rosemary

Directions

1. In the bread machine pan, place the water, 2 tbsp of the olive oil, salt, garlic, 1 tbsp of the rosemary, bread flour and yeast in the order recommended by the manufacturer.
2. Select the Dough cycle and press Start.
3. After the cycle is completed, remove the dough and pat into a 13x9-inch baking pan.
4. With your fingers, dimple the dough every inch.
5. Coat with the remaining olive oil and sprinkle with the remaining rosemary.
6. Set your oven to 400 degrees F.
7. Cover focaccia with plastic wrap while oven preheats.
8. Cook in the oven for about 20-25 minutes.
9. Let it cool for 5 minutes before serving.

Rustic
Basil Oregano and Rosemary Bread

🍳 Prep Time: 10 mins
🕐 Total Time: 3 hrs 10 mins

Servings per Recipe: 8	
Calories	234 kcal
Fat	4.6 g
Carbohydrates	41.2g
Protein	6.3 g
Cholesterol	23 mg
Sodium	302 mg

Ingredients

1 C. warm water
1 egg, beaten
1 tsp salt
2 tbsp white sugar
2 tbsp extra-virgin olive oil
2 tsp dried rosemary leaves, crushed

1 tsp dried oregano
1 tsp dried basil
3 C. all-purpose flour
2 tbsp all-purpose flour
2 tsp bread machine yeast

Directions

1. In the bread machine pan, place the warm water.
2. Add the remaining ingredients in the order recommended by the manufacturer.
3. Set the machine to bake a large loaf with the Light Crust and press Start.

EASTERN EUROPEAN
Sweet Buns (Kolaches)

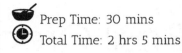 Prep Time: 30 mins

Total Time: 2 hrs 5 mins

Servings per Recipe: 24

Calories	216 kcal
Fat	7.8 g
Carbohydrates	31.7g
Protein	4.6 g
Cholesterol	32 mg
Sodium	164 mg

Ingredients

1 1/4 C. warm water
1/2 C. butter, softened
1 egg
1 egg yolk
1/3 C. milk powder
1/4 C. instant mashed potato flakes
1/4 C. white sugar
1 tsp salt

3 7/8 C. bread flour
2 tsp active dry yeast
1 (12 oz.) can cherry pie filling
1 (12 oz.) can poppy seed filling
1/4 C. butter, melted

Directions

1. In the bread machine pan, place the water, softened butter, egg, egg yolk, milk powder, potato flakes, sugar, salt, flour and yeast in the order recommended by the manufacturer.
2. Select the Dough cycle and press Start.
3. Check dough after 5 minutes of mixing, adding 1-2 tbsp of the water if required.
4. After the cycle is completes, spoon out the dough with a tbsp and roll into walnut sized balls.
5. Place the balls onto a lightly greased cookie sheet about 2-inches apart.
6. Cover and keep in the warm place for about 1 hour.
7. With the palm of your hand, flatten the balls slightly and with your thumb, make a depression in center.
8. Fill the depression with 1 tbsp of the filling.
9. Cover and keep in the warm place for about 30 minutes.
10. Set your oven to 375 degrees F.
11. Cook in the oven for about 13-15 minutes.
12. Remove from the oven and coat with the melted butter.
13. Cool on wire rack.

Honey
Spelt Bread

Prep Time: 10 mins
Total Time: 1 hr 30 mins

Servings per Recipe: 12
Calories	118 kcal
Fat	1.3 g
Carbohydrates	23g
Protein	4.9 g
Cholesterol	1 mg
Sodium	302 mg

Ingredients

1 C. water
1 1/2 tsp vegetable oil
1 1/2 tsp honey
1/2 tsp lecithin
3 C. white spelt flour
3 tbsp dry milk powder

1 1/2 tsp salt
2 tsp active dry yeast

Directions

1. In the bread machine pan, place all the ingredients in the order recommended by the manufacturer.
2. Set the Normal or Basic cycle and press Start.

PUMPERNICKEL
at Home

🥣 Prep Time: 10 mins
🕐 Total Time: 3 hrs 55 mins

Servings per Recipe: 12

Calories	181 kcal
Fat	2.6 g
Carbohydrates	34.8g
Protein	5.5 g
Cholesterol	0 mg
Sodium	296 mg

Ingredients

1 1/8 C. warm water
1 1/2 tbsp vegetable oil
1/3 C. molasses
3 tbsp cocoa
1 tbsp caraway seed (optional)
1 1/2 tsp salt
1 1/2 C. bread flour
1 C. rye flour

1 C. whole wheat flour
1 1/2 tbsp vital wheat gluten (optional)
2 1/2 tsp bread machine yeast

Directions

1. In the bread machine pan, place all the ingredients in the order recommended by the manufacturer.
2. Set the Basic cycle and press Start.

Back to School
Bread

Prep Time: 5 mins
Total Time: 3 hrs

Servings per Recipe: 10
Calories	162 kcal
Fat	3.2 g
Carbohydrates	27.8g
Protein	4.8 g
Cholesterol	2 mg
Sodium	234 mg

Ingredients

7 fluid oz. warm water (110 degrees F/45 degrees C)
2 tbsp lard
1 (.25 oz.) package active dry yeast

2 3/4 C. bread flour
1 tsp salt
1 tsp ground cinnamon (optional)

Directions

1. In the bread machine pan, place the warm water and lard.
2. Sprinkle with the yeast.
3. Place the flour, salt and toss in the cinnamon.
4. Select the cycle and press Start.

BREAD MACHINE
Cake

🥣 Prep Time: 15 mins
🕐 Total Time: 3 hrs 55 mins

Servings per Recipe: 10	
Calories	184 kcal
Fat	6.3 g
Carbohydrates	27.9g
Protein	4.3 g
Cholesterol	24 mg
Sodium	254 mg

Ingredients

1 (1.1 oz.) package chai tea powder
3/4 C. hot water
1/4 C. Chardonnay wine
1/2 tsp vanilla extract
1 egg yolk
1/2 C. frozen unsweetened raspberries
1 tbsp butter, room temperature
1/2 C. bread flour
1/4 C. rye flour

1 C. all-purpose flour
1/2 C. wheat bran
1 (.25 oz.) package active dry yeast
1/2 C. coarsely chopped walnuts
1/2 tsp caraway seed
1/4 C. white sugar
1 tsp coarse smoked salt flakes

Directions

1. In a cup, add 3/4 C. of the hot water and chai tea powder package and stir to combine.
2. Keep aside to cool for about 10 minutes.
3. In the bread machine pan, mix together the chai tea, Chardonnay, vanilla extract, egg yolk, frozen raspberries and butter.
4. Add the bread flour, rye flour, all-purpose flour, wheat bran, yeast, walnuts, caraway seed, sugar and salt.
5. Select the Sweet setting with a Light Crust and press Start.
6. After the baking is completed, let it cool for at least 30 minutes before slicing and serving.

Louie Cake

Prep Time: 20 mins
Total Time: 3 hrs 25 mins

Servings per Recipe: 14
Calories	315 kcal
Fat	11.9 g
Carbohydrates	47.8g
Protein	5 g
Cholesterol	34 mg
Sodium	134 mg

Ingredients

1/4 C. warm water (100 to 110 degrees F/40 to 45 degrees C)
1/2 tsp salt
2 tbsp softened butter
1 egg, slightly beaten
1 C. sour cream
3 1/2 tbsp white sugar
3 1/2 C. all-purpose flour
2 1/2 tsp active dry yeast
1/4 C. white sugar
1 tsp ground cinnamon
2 1/2 tbsp melted butter

1/2 C. chopped pecans
1 1/2 C. confectioners' sugar
1 1/2 tbsp melted butter
1/8 tsp vanilla extract
2 tbsp milk
1 tbsp purple colored sugar
1 tbsp green colored sugar
1 tbsp yellow colored sugar

Directions

1. In the bread machine pan, place the warm water, salt, softened butter, egg, sour cream, 3 1/2 tbsp of sugar, flour and yeast in the order recommended by the manufacturer.
2. Select the Dough cycle and press Start.
3. Check the dough after about 5 minutes of mixing, and add 1-2 tbsp of water or flour if the dough is too dry or wet.
4. In a bowl, mix together 1/4 C. of the sugar, cinnamon and 2 1/2 tbsp of the melted butter.
5. Grease a baking sheet and keep aside.
6. After the dough cycle is completed, transfer the dough onto a floured surface and roll into a 10x28-inch rectangle.
7. Spread the butter mixture over the dough and sprinkle with the pecans in an even layer.
8. Pick up one of the long edges, and roll the dough into a 28-inch long log.

9. Place the rolled dough onto the prepared baking sheet, seam side down and shape the dough into a ring.
10. With wet fingers, moisten the ends of the dough slightly and pinch the two ends together to seal.
11. With a cloth, cover the dough ring and keep in a warm place for about 30 minutes.
12. Set your oven to 375 degrees F.
13. Cook in the oven for about 15 minutes.
14. In a bowl, mix together the confectioners' sugar, 1 1/2 tbsp of the melted butter, vanilla extract and enough milk to make a smooth glaze.
15. Remove the cake from the oven and cool for about 10 minutes on a wire rack.
16. Place the glaze over the warm cake, allowing drips of glaze to dribble down the sides of the cake.
17. Immediately sprinkle the cake with the bands of purple, green and yellow colored sugar.
18. Allow the cake to cool completely before serving.

Artisanal
White Bread

Prep Time: 5 mins
Total Time: 3 hrs 5 mins

Servings per Recipe: 12
Calories	168 kcal
Fat	4 g
Carbohydrates	28.3g
Protein	4.4 g
Cholesterol	0 mg
Sodium	292 mg

Ingredients

1 C. warm water (110 degrees F/45 degrees C)
3 tbsp white sugar
1 1/2 tsp salt

3 tbsp vegetable oil
3 C. bread flour
2 1/4 tsp active dry yeast

Directions

1. In the bread machine pan, place all the ingredients in the order recommended by the manufacturer.
2. Select the White Bread setting.
3. Cool on wire racks before slicing.

FLAVORSOME
Bread Machine Bread

Prep Time: 10 mins
Total Time: 3 hrs 10 mins

Servings per Recipe: 12
Calories   142 kcal
Fat   1.6 g
Carbohydrates   26.9g
Protein   4.7 g
Cholesterol   3 mg
Sodium   303 mg

Ingredients

1 C. warm water (110 degrees F)
1 tbsp butter
1 tbsp dry milk powder
1 tbsp white sugar
1 1/2 tsp salt
1 1/2 tbsp dried parsley

2 tsp garlic powder
3 C. bread flour
2 tsp active dry yeast

Directions

1. In the bread machine pan, place all the ingredients in the order recommended by the manufacturer.
2. Select the Basic Bread cycle and press Start.

Bread
Bolognese

Prep Time: 20 mins
Total Time: 3 hrs 20 mins

Servings per Recipe: 20
Calories   105 kcal
Fat   0.9 g
Carbohydrates   20.6 g
Protein   3.1 g
Cholesterol   9 mg
Sodium   179 mg

Ingredients

4 C. unbleached all-purpose flour
1 tbsp light brown sugar
1 1/3 C. warm water (110 degrees F / 45 degrees C)
1 1/2 tsp salt
1 1/2 tsp olive oil

1 (.25 oz.) package active dry yeast
1 egg
1 tbsp water
2 tbsp cornmeal

Directions

1. In the bread machine pan, place the flour, brown sugar, warm water, salt, olive oil and yeast in the order recommended by the manufacturer.
2. Select the Dough cycle and press Start.
3. Deflate the dough and transfer onto a lightly floured surface.
4. Shape the dough into two equal sized loaves.
5. Place the loaves, seam side down on a cutting board, sprinkled with the cornmeal generously.
6. With a damp cloth, cover the loaves and keep in warm place for about 40 minutes.
7. Set your oven to 375 degrees F.
8. In a small bowl, add the egg and 1 tbsp of the water and beat well.
9. Coat the loaves with the egg mixture and with a sharp knife, make a single long, quick cut down the center of the loaves.
10. Carefully, place the loaves onto a baking sheet
11. Cook in the oven for about 30-35 minutes.

WALNUTS
and Cinnamon Swirl

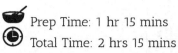 Prep Time: 1 hr 15 mins
Total Time: 2 hrs 15 mins

Servings per Recipe: 24	
Calories	162 kcal
Fat	5.5 g
Carbohydrates	24.4g
Protein	4.1 g
Cholesterol	24 mg
Sodium	129 mg

Ingredients

1 C. milk
2 eggs
1/4 C. butter
4 C. bread flour
1/4 C. white sugar
1 tsp salt
1 1/2 tsp active dry yeast
1/2 C. chopped walnuts

1/2 C. packed brown sugar
2 tsp ground cinnamon
2 tbsp softened butter, divided
2 tsp sifted confectioners' sugar, divided
(optional)

Directions

1. In the bread machine pan, place the milk, eggs, 1/4 C. of the butter, bread flour, sugar, salt, and yeast in the order recommended by the manufacturer.
2. Select the Dough setting and press Start.
3. After the dough cycle is completed, transfer the dough onto a floured surface and punch down.
4. Let the dough rest for about 10 minutes.
5. In a bowl, mix together walnuts, brown sugar and cinnamon.
6. Divide the dough in half and roll each half into a 9x14-inches rectangle.
7. Spread 1 tbsp of the softened butter over the top of each dough rectangle evenly and sprinkle with half of the walnut mixture.
8. Roll dough rectangles, starting from the short ends, and pinch seams closed.
9. Grease 2 (9x5-inch) loaf pans.
10. Place the rolled loaves into the prepared loaf pans, seam sides down.
11. Cover and keep in warm place for about 30 minutes.
12. Set your oven to 350 degrees F.

13. Cook in the oven for about 30 minutes.
14. Let the breads cool in the pans for about 10 minutes before removing to finish cooling on wire racks.
15. Sprinkle each loaf with 1 tsp of the confectioners' sugar.

CARDAMOM
Pearl Sugar
Coffee Bread

 Prep Time: 15 mins

Total Time: 2 hrs 40 mins

Servings per Recipe: 8	
Calories	283 kcal
Fat	4.6 g
Carbohydrates	52.8g
Protein	7.5 g
Cholesterol	36 mg
Sodium	195 mg

Ingredients

1 C. milk

1/2 tsp salt

1 egg yolk

2 tbsp softened butter

3 C. all-purpose flour

1/3 C. sugar

1 (.25 oz.) envelope active dry yeast

3 tsp ground cardamom

2 egg whites, slightly beaten

pearl sugar

Directions

1. In the bread machine pan, place all the ingredients in the order recommended by the manufacturer.
2. Select the Dough cycle and press Start.
3. After the dough cycle is completed, divide into 3 equal portions.
4. Roll each portion into a 12-14-inches long rope.
5. Place the three ropes side by side, then braid together.
6. Tuck the ends underneath and place onto a greased baking sheet.
7. With a towel, cover loosely and keep in warm place to rise till doubled in size.
8. Set your oven to 375 degrees F.
9. Coat the loaf with the beaten egg and sprinkle with the pearl sugar.
10. Cook in the oven for about 20-25 minutes.

Buttermilk
Maple Bread

Prep Time: 1 hr 30 mins
Total Time: 3 d 11 h 20 m

Servings per Recipe: 15

Calories	104 kcal
Fat	0.9 g
Carbohydrates	20.6 g
Protein	4.9 g
Cholesterol	13 mg
Sodium	124 mg

Ingredients

1/2 C. sprouted wheat berries, ground
3/4 C. buttermilk
1 egg
2 tbsp maple syrup
1/2 tsp salt
1/3 tsp baking soda

2 tbsp vital wheat gluten
2 1/4 C. whole wheat flour
1 1/2 tsp active dry yeast

Directions

1. Rinse 1/2 C. of the raw wheat berries in cool water and drain.
2. In a large bowl of the water, add the berries and soak, covered for 12 hours or overnight.
3. In a colander, drain the berries and keep, covered in a dark place.
4. Rinse for about 3 times a day and they will soon begin to sprout.
5. In a couple of days the sprouts will reach their optimum length of about 1/4-inch.
6. Drain the sprouts and in a food processor, grind them.
7. In the bread machine pan, place all the ingredients in the order recommended by the manufacturer.
8. Select the Whole Wheat cycle and Medium Crust setting and press Start.

RESTAURANT STYLE
Bread

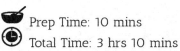

Prep Time: 10 mins
Total Time: 3 hrs 10 mins

Servings per Recipe: 8
Calories   167 kcal
Fat   2.1 g
Carbohydrates   34.2g
Protein   4.5 g
Cholesterol   4 mg
Sodium   158 mg

Ingredients

3/4 C. warm water
1 tbsp butter, softened
1/4 C. honey
1/2 tsp salt
1 tsp instant coffee granules
1 tbsp unsweetened cocoa powder

1 tbsp white sugar
1 C. bread flour
1 C. whole wheat flour
1 1/4 tsp bread machine yeast

Directions

1. In the bread machine pan, place all the ingredients in the order recommended by the manufacturer.
2. Select the Regular or Basic cycle with Light Crust and press Start.

New York City
Inspired Bread

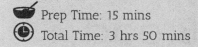 Prep Time: 15 mins

Total Time: 3 hrs 50 mins

Servings per Recipe: 10	
Calories	215 kcal
Fat	6.2 g
Carbohydrates	32.8g
Protein	6.6 g
Cholesterol	37 mg
Sodium	417 mg

Ingredients

1 C. warm water (110 degrees F / 45 degrees C)
1 1/2 tsp salt
2 tbsp white sugar
1/4 C. pareve margarine
1 egg

3 C. bread flour
2 1/4 tsp bread machine yeast
1 egg
1 tbsp water
1/8 tsp vanilla extract

Directions

1. In the bread machine pan, place the warm water, salt, sugar, margarine, egg, bread flour and yeast.
2. Set the Dough setting and press Start.
3. After the dough cycle is completed, transfer the dough onto a floured surface.
4. Divide the dough into 3 portions and roll each into about 12-inches long ropes.
5. Pinch 3 ropes together at the top and braid them.
6. Starting with the strand to the right, move it to the left over the middle strand.
7. Take the strand farthest to the left and move it over the new middle strand.
8. Keep braiding, alternating sides each time, until the loaf is braided, and pinch the ends together and fold them underneath for a neat look.
9. Place the braided challah onto a greased baking sheet.
10. With a plastic wrap, cover the loaf and keep in a warm place for about 1 hour.
11. Set your oven to 350 degrees F.
12. In a small bowl, add 1 egg, 1 tbsp of the water and vanilla extract and beat till well combined.
13. Coat the egg glaze over the challah and sprinkle with desired toppings.
14. Cook in the oven for about 35-40 minutes.

SUNDAY'S
Bread

Prep Time: 20 mins
Total Time: 2 hrs 20 mins

Servings per Recipe: 14
Calories	193 kcal
Fat	6.1 g
Carbohydrates	30.8g
Protein	6.2 g
Cholesterol	40 mg
Sodium	299 mg

Ingredients

1 C. warm water
1/4 C. olive oil
2 eggs
1 1/2 tsp salt
1/3 C. white sugar
2 C. white spelt flour

2 C. whole grain spelt flour
4 tsp xanthan gum
1 (.25 oz.) envelope dry yeast
1 egg, beaten
1 tbsp poppy seeds

Directions

1. In the bread machine pan, place the water, olive oil, eggs, salt, sugar, spelt flours, xanthan gum and yeast.
2. Set the Dough cycle.
3. After the cycle is completed, remove the dough and divide into 3 portions.
4. Shape each portion into an 18-inch long rope.
5. Braid the three ropes together.
6. Seal the tips together and fold under the loaf.
7. Place the braided loaf onto a greased baking sheet.
8. With a soft cloth, cover and keep in warm place for about 1 hour.
9. Set your oven to 375 degrees F.
10. Coat the loaf with the beaten egg and sprinkle with the poppy seeds.
11. Cook in the oven for about 40-45 minutes.

Oats
and Pickle Bread

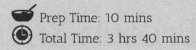 Prep Time: 10 mins
Total Time: 3 hrs 40 mins

Servings per Recipe: 16	
Calories	178 kcal
Fat	3.6 g
Carbohydrates	32g
Protein	5.1 g
Cholesterol	0 mg
Sodium	113 mg

Ingredients

1 1/2 C. pickle juice
1/2 C. water
3 tbsp vegetable oil
3/4 tsp salt
3 1/2 tbsp white sugar
1/2 C. wheat germ

3/4 C. rolled oats
1 1/4 C. whole wheat flour
3 C. all-purpose flour
1 tsp active dry yeast

Directions

1. In the bread machine pan, place the dill pickle juice, water, vegetable oil, salt, white sugar, wheat germ, oats, whole wheat flour, all-purpose flour, and yeast.
2. Select the Sandwich and 3-lb. Loaf settings and press Start.
3. Cycle should take about 3 hours 10 minutes to complete.
4. Remove the loaf from the bread pan and let it cool on wire rack for at least 20 minutes before slicing.

BUTTERMILK
Brown Sugar Bread Rolls

 Prep Time: 15 mins
Total Time: 2 hrs 35 mins

Servings per Recipe: 12
Calories	176 kcal
Fat	4.4 g
Carbohydrates	28.3g
Protein	5.2 g
Cholesterol	20 mg
Sodium	271 mg

Ingredients

3 C. bread flour

1 C. buttermilk

2 tbsp packed brown sugar

1 1/2 tsp kosher salt

1 (.25 oz.) package active dry yeast

1 egg yolk

2 tbsp canola oil

stick butter

Directions

1. In the bread machine pan, place the bread flour, buttermilk, brown sugar, salt, yeast and egg yolk.

2. Select the Dough setting and let the machine to mix the ingredients till moist.

3. Pause the cycle and add the oil, then let the machine continue to the end of the Dough cycle.

4. Grease the cups of the muffin pans and keep aside.

5. Punch down the dough and remove it from the machine.

6. Divide the dough into 12 equal portions and shape into round, smooth rolls.

7. Arrange the rolls into the prepared muffin cups.

8. Cover the rolls with a kitchen towel and keep in the warm place for about 25 minutes.

9. Set your oven to 350 degrees F.

10. Cook in the oven for about 20 minutes.

11. Remove from the oven and immediately, rub the tops of the hot rolls with a stick of the butter for a soft crust.

12. Cool the rolls slightly and serve warm.

Pizza Crust II

Servings per Recipe: 8	
Calories	163 kcal
Fat	4.1 g
Carbohydrates	28.3g
Protein	5.5 g
Cholesterol	0 mg
Sodium	294 mg

Ingredients

1 C. warm water (110 degrees F/45 degrees C)
1 (.25 oz.) package active dry yeast
1 tsp white sugar
2 1/2 C. whole wheat flour
2 tbsp olive oil

1 1/2 tsp dried basil
1 1/2 tsp dried oregano
1 tsp salt

Directions

1. In the bread machine pan, mix together the water, yeast, and sugar and let it stand for about 10 minutes.
2. Place the flour, olive oil, basil, oregano and salt over the yeast mixture.
3. Place bread machine bowl in the bread machine.
4. Select the Dough setting and press Start.

RYE BREAD
101

Prep Time: 5 mins
Total Time: 3 hrs 5 mins

Servings per Recipe: 12

Calories	198 kcal
Fat	3.3 g
Carbohydrates	36.8g
Protein	6.6 g
Cholesterol	0 mg
Sodium	197 mg

Ingredients

1 1/2 C. water
3 tbsp honey
2 tbsp olive oil
3 tsp caraway seed
1/2 C. cornmeal
1 1/2 C. dark rye flour

2 C. bread flour
2 tbsp vital wheat gluten
2 tsp active dry yeast
1 tsp salt

Directions

1. In the bread machine pan, place all the ingredients in the order recommended by the manufacturer.
2. Set for French bread cycle or Normal setting.

Olive oil
Wheat Bread

Prep Time: 15 mins
Total Time: 1 hr 15 mins

Servings per Recipe: 15
Calories   109 kcal
Fat   1.3 g
Carbohydrates   21g
Protein   3.8 g
Cholesterol   1 mg
Sodium   86 mg

Ingredients

1 (.25 oz.) package active dry yeast
1 C. skim milk, luke warm
2 tbsp warm water (110 degrees F/45 degrees C)
1/2 tsp salt
2 C. all-purpose flour

1 1/4 C. whole wheat flour
1 tbsp olive oil

Directions

1. In the bread machine pan, place all the ingredients in the order recommended by the manufacturer.
2. Select the Lightest setting and press Start.

BUSH
Bread

Prep Time: 10 mins
Total Time: 3 hrs 10 mins

Servings per Recipe: 6

Calories	319 kcal
Fat	7.5 g
Carbohydrates	55.1g
Protein	7.2 g
Cholesterol	0 mg
Sodium	585 mg

Ingredients

1 C. warm water (110 degrees F (43 degrees C))
2 1/2 tsp active dry yeast
3 tbsp white sugar
1 1/2 tsp salt
3 tbsp olive oil

1/2 tsp ground thyme
1/2 tsp garlic powder
2 tsp crushed dried rosemary
3 C. all-purpose flour

Directions

1. In the bread machine pan, add the water and sprinkle with the yeast and sugar.
2. Let the mixture sit in the bread machine for about 10 minutes.
3. Sprinkle the salt, then add the olive oil, thyme, garlic powder, rosemary and flour.
4. Set the machine for Light Crust setting and press Start.

Simple
Banana Bread

Prep Time: 15 mins
Total Time: 1 hr 15 mins

Servings per Recipe: 10

Calories	221 kcal
Fat	5.4 g
Carbohydrates	39.7g
Protein	4.1 g
Cholesterol	37 mg
Sodium	126 mg

Ingredients

2 C. all-purpose flour
1 tsp baking powder
1/2 tsp baking soda
3/4 C. white sugar

3 tbsp vegetable oil
2 eggs
2 bananas, peeled and halved lengthwise

Directions

1. In the bread machine pan, place all the ingredients in the order recommended by the manufacturer.
2. Select the Dough setting and press Start.
3. Mix the bread for about 3-5 minutes till the bananas are mashed and all ingredients are combined completely.
4. Press the Stop.
5. With a rubber spatula, smooth the top of the loaf.
6. Select the Bake setting and press Start.
7. The Bake cycle time will be about 50 minutes or till a toothpick inserted into the center comes out clean.
8. Remove the pan from the machine but keep the bread in the pan for about 10 minutes.
9. Remove the bread to cool completely on a wire rack.

CARAWAY
and Molasses Bread

Prep Time: 10 mins
Total Time: 4 hrs 10 mins

Servings per Recipe: 12
Calories   165 kcal
Fat   2.6 g
Carbohydrates   31g
Protein   4.8 g
Cholesterol   5 mg
Sodium   218 mg

Ingredients

1 1/4 C. lukewarm water (100 degrees
F/38 degrees C)
2 tbsp dry milk powder
1 tsp salt
2 tbsp brown sugar
2 tbsp molasses
2 tbsp butter

3/4 C. whole wheat flour
1 3/4 C. bread flour
3/4 C. rye flour
1 1/2 tbsp caraway seeds
1 3/4 tsp active dry yeast

Directions

1. In the bread machine pan, place all the ingredients in the order recommended by the manufacturer.
2. Select the Grain setting and 2-lb. loaf size.

Honey and Oats

Prep Time: 10 mins
Total Time: 3 hrs 15 mins

Servings per Recipe: 12
Calories   281 kcal
Fat   8.9 g
Carbohydrates   44.7g
Protein   6.4 g
Cholesterol   10 mg
Sodium   225 mg

Ingredients

2 1/2 tsp active dry yeast
2 tbsp white sugar
1 1/2 C. warm water (110 degrees F/45 degrees C)
3 C. all-purpose flour
1 C. whole wheat flour
1 C. rolled oats
3 tbsp powdered milk

1 tsp salt
1/4 C. honey
1/4 C. vegetable oil
3 tbsp butter, softened
cooking spray

Directions

1. In the bread machine pan, place the yeast, sugar, and water.
2. Let the yeast to dissolve and foam for about 10 minutes.
3. Meanwhile in a bowl, mix together the all-purpose flour, whole wheat flour, rolled oats, powdered milk and salt.
4. In the yeast mixture, add the honey, vegetable oil and butter and top with the flour mixture.
5. Select the Dough cycle and press Start.
6. Allow the bread machine to complete the cycle for about 1 1/2 hours.
7. Now, transfer the dough to a 9x5-inch greased loaf pan and keep in warm place for about 1 hour.
8. Set your oven to 375 degrees F.
9. Cook in the oven for about 35 minutes.

COCOA
Bread

Prep Time: 10 mins
Total Time: 3 hrs 50 mins

Servings per Recipe: 12
Calories	259 kcal
Fat	7.3 g
Carbohydrates	38.3g
Protein	8.3 g
Cholesterol	17 mg
Sodium	260 mg

Ingredients

1/4 C. water
1 C. milk
1 egg
1 tbsp vanilla extract
3 1/3 C. bread flour
1/4 C. sucralose and brown sugar blend
(such as Splenda(R) brown sugar blend)
1 tsp salt
1 tsp ground cinnamon

1 tsp cocoa powder (such as
Hershey's(R))
1 1/2 tsp active dry yeast
2 tbsp margarine, softened
1/2 C. peanut butter chips (such as
Reese's(R))
1/4 C. semisweet chocolate chips

Directions

1. In the bread machine pan, place the water, milk, egg, vanilla extract, bread flour, sucralose and brown sugar blend, salt, cinnamon, cocoa powder, yeast and margarine in the order recommended by the manufacturer.

2. Select a 1 1/2-lb. loaf cycle with a Light Crust and press Start.

3. Add the peanut butter chips and semisweet chocolate chips when the final knead cycle begins.

4. Cool the bread for about 10-15 minutes before slicing.

December's
Orange Yogurt Bread

🥣 Prep Time: 5 mins
🕐 Total Time: 3 hrs 5 mins

Servings per Recipe: 12
Calories	180 kcal
Fat	1.5 g
Carbohydrates	37.8g
Protein	4.3 g
Cholesterol	3 mg
Sodium	310 mg

Ingredients

3 C. all-purpose flour
1 C. dried cranberries
3/4 C. plain yogurt
1/2 C. warm water
3 tbsp honey
1 tbsp butter, melted

2 tsp active dry yeast
1 1/2 tsp salt
1 tsp orange oil

Directions

1. In the bread machine pan, place them in the order recommended by the manufacturer.
2. Select the Light Crust setting and press Start.

NO GLUTEN
Potato Honey Bread

Prep Time: 10 mins
Total Time: 1 hr 30 mins

Servings per Recipe: 12
Calories	242 kcal
Fat	6.7 g
Carbohydrates	39.6 g
Protein	6.3 g
Cholesterol	48 mg
Sodium	275 mg

Ingredients

3 eggs
1 tbsp cider vinegar
1/4 C. olive oil
1/4 C. honey
1 1/2 C. buttermilk, at room temperature
1 tsp salt

1 tbsp xanthan gum
1/3 C. cornstarch
1/2 C. potato starch
1/2 C. soy flour
2 C. white rice flour
1 tbsp active dry yeast

Directions

1. In the bread machine pan, place them in the order recommended by the manufacturer.
2. Select the Sweet Dough cycle.
3. Five minutes into the cycle, check the consistency of the dough. (Add additional rice flour or liquid if necessary.)
4. When bread is finished, let it cool for about 10-15 minutes before removing from pan.

ENJOY THE RECIPES?

KEEP ON COOKING
WITH 6 MORE FREE COOKBOOKS!

Visit our website and simply enter your email address to join the club and receive your 6 cookbooks.

http://booksumo.com/magnet

https://www.instagram.com/booksumopress/

https://www.facebook.com/booksumo/

Made in the USA
Monee, IL
23 March 2020

23786922R10050